Great Moments in
Olympic
SKATING

By Jo-Ann Barnas

Great
Moments in
OLYMPIC
SPORTS

SportsZone

An Imprint of Abdo Publishing
www.abdopublishing.com

www.abdopublishing.com

Published by Abdo Publishing, a division of ABDO, PO Box 398166, Minneapolis, Minnesota 55439. Copyright © 2015 by Abdo Consulting Group, Inc. International copyrights reserved in all countries. No part of this book may be reproduced in any form without written permission from the publisher. SportsZone™ is a trademark and logo of Abdo Publishing.

Printed in the United States of America, North Mankato, Minnesota
042014
092014

Cover Photo: Lionel Cironneau/AP Images
Interior Photos: Lionel Cironneau/AP Images, 1, 49; Chris Trotman/Duomo/Corbis, 6–7; AP Images, 9, 14–15, 17, 21, 22–23, 27; Roberto Borea/AP Images, 13; Ed Andrieski/AP Images, 28–29; John Redman/AP Images, 31; Jack Smith/AP Images, 33; Gilbert Iundt/Jean-Yves Ruszniewski/TempSport/Corbis, 35; Thomas Kienzle/AP Images, 36–37; Mark Duncan/AP Images, 40; John Gaps III/AP Images, 43; Jae C. Hong/AP Images, 44–45; Amy Sancetta/AP Images, 51, 52–53; Mark Baker/AP Images, 55, 58

Editor: Chrös McDougall
Series Designer: Craig Hinton

Library of Congress Control Number: 2014932872

Cataloging-in-Publication Data
Barnas, Jo-Ann.
 Great moments in Olympic skating / Jo-Ann Barnas.
   p. cm. -- (Great moments in Olympic sports)
Includes bibliographical references and index.
ISBN 978-1-62403-396-4
1. Skating--Juvenile literature. 2. Figure skating--Juvenile literature. 3. Ice skating--Juvenile literature. 4. Winter Olympics--Juvenile literature.   I. Title.
796.91--dc23

                                                      2014932872

Contents

Introduction

The first modern ice skaters might have been from the Netherlands. People there skated on frozen canals as early as the thirteenth century. Over the years, the practice spread to other countries.

Skaters in Scotland were tracing figures on the ice by the 1600s. In the 1860s, an American named Jackson Haines introduced elements of dance to the sport we know today as figure skating. The first Olympic Winter Games were held in 1924. However, figure skating was first contested at the 1908 Summer Olympics. It has been a regular part of the Olympic program since 1920. Olympic figure skating has always included divisions for men, women, and pairs. Ice dancing was added in 1976. A new team event debuted at the 2014 Winter Games.

In figure skating, each singles skater, pairs team, or ice dancing team performs twice in a competition. The first event is called a short program. The second is called a freestyle long program, or free skate.

Speedskating developed out of the Dutch mode of transportation. Long-track speedskating became an Olympic sport at the first Winter Games in 1924. Two athletes per heat race against the clock on a 400-meter oval. Today's Olympic program includes five individual events for both men and women. They range from 500 to 10,000 meters. Men and women each compete in a team pursuit race as well.

Short-track speedskating was added to the Olympics in 1992. It takes place on a 111-meter oval. Athletes race in a pack, which leads to exciting maneuvers. Men and women each have three individual events ranging from 500 to 1,500 meters, plus a team relay.

Salt Lake City 2002
SARAH'S BIG SURPRISE

Sarah Hughes was a long way from winning when she went to sleep the night after the short program at the 2002 Olympic Winter Games in Salt Lake City, Utah. She had ended the first night of competition in fourth place. No one had ever come back to win the Olympic title in women's figure skating from that position. It seemed impossible. Especially for her.

Going into the Olympics, not many thought Hughes could capture a medal, let alone win gold. At only 16, she struggled just to make the US team. Hughes had taken

American Sarah Hughes performs in the short program at the 2002 Olympic Winter Games in Salt Lake City, Utah.

Sarah Hughes skates in the long program at the 2002
Olympic Winter Games.

the third and final US spot after winning the bronze medal at the national championships. The other two American figure skaters, Michelle Kwan and Sasha Cohen, were considered better.

Kwan, 21, was the top skater in the world. She had won six US championships and four world titles heading into the 2002 Winter Games. But she had never won an Olympic gold medal. Kwan finished runner-up to gold medalist Tara Lipinski at the 1998 Winter Games in Nagano, Japan. The 17-year-old Cohen, meanwhile, was a two-time US medalist at the time.

Hughes was the underdog. But she didn't mind. She loved competing. When she was a little girl, she kept a cereal box as a souvenir in her bedroom. On the cover was her role model: 1992 Olympic champion Kristi Yamaguchi.

Hughes grew up on Long Island in New York with five brothers and sisters who were as active as she was. One of her sisters, Emily, was also a figure skater. In fact, Emily Hughes would finish seventh at the 2006 Winter Games in Turin, Italy. Sarah was active in other ways, too. When she was in middle school, she played violin in the orchestra. Then she became an honor student in high school. After the Olympics, she attended college at Yale University.

An Olympic Underdog

At the 2002 Olympics, Hughes wasn't at her best in the short program. She made mistakes on two triple jumps when she under-rotated them. When that part of the competition ended, ahead of Hughes in the standings were familiar rivals: Kwan, Irina Slutskaya of Russia, and Cohen. The gold medal seemed out of reach.

But Hughes's coach Robin Wagner was confident. She knew that Hughes had taken the month going into the Olympics to work hard on her jumps.

"The US has an incredibly strong team," Wagner said. "I'd love to see our girls finish 1-2-3. Obviously, you can figure out which order my favorite on the podium would be."

The long program was held two days after the short program. Wearing a sparkling lavender skating dress, Hughes looked confident as she glided to center ice. A fan held up a sign in the packed arena.

"You Go Girl," it said.

Hughes landed her first jump, a double Axel. An Axel is one of the most difficult jumps because the skater takes off from a forward position. Then she nailed a difficult triple-triple combination. A minute later, when she added another triple-triple combination, fans could hardly believe what she had done. Hughes had just become the first female skater in Olympic history to land two triple-triple combinations.

As her four-minute routine went on, she got stronger and faster. She attempted seven total triple jumps and landed all of them. On her layback spin, she looked like a music box ballerina. When her routine ended, she doubled over with joy.

But the competition wasn't finished yet. In order for Hughes to win, Slutskaya had to finish ahead of Kwan, who had to finish ahead of Cohen. But that was exactly what happened. Kwan settled for the bronze medal after making mistakes on two jumps. She fell one time. Cohen fell once, too. She took fourth place. Slutskaya skated like she was very nervous.

Falling Short

Michelle Kwan was one of the most accomplished figure skaters of all time. The one thing she did not accomplish, however, was an Olympic gold medal. Outside of the Olympics, she won nine US championships between 1996 and 2005. She also won five world titles between 1996 and 2003. No US woman had won more through 2014. In both of Kwan's Olympics, though, an upstart American stepped up to win gold. Kwan finished second at the 1998 Olympics. Her rival, Tara Lipinski, became the youngest Olympic figure skating gold medalist at 15. Four years later in 2002, Sarah Hughes shocked fans by winning the gold medal while Kwan settled for third. Kwan also qualified for the 2006 Olympics but was unable to go because of an injury.

She didn't try any of her triple-triple combinations. The Russian took second in the long program and won the silver medal.

"I think a lot of people counted me out and didn't think I could do it," Hughes said. "I didn't even think it would be possible. So just to be sitting here with this medal around my neck, I didn't think it could happen."

Hughes's victory was exciting for the sport. She became the first American figure skater to win the Olympic title without having won either a world or US senior title. She also became the seventh US Olympic gold medalist following Tara Lipinski (1998), Kristi Yamaguchi (1992), Dorothy Hamill (1976), Peggy Fleming (1968), Carol Heiss (1960), and Tenley Albright (1956).

How happy was Sarah? When her marks popped up on the scoreboard, the figure skater looked at her coach and said with a big smile: "Let's do it again!"

St. Moritz 1948
AN AMERICAN ORIGINAL

Dick Button loved to jump. He loved it more than anything else. That showed at the 1948 Olympic Winter Games in St. Moritz, Switzerland. Button was so good that he landed a jump that changed the sport of figure skating. The trick was called a double Axel. It's a forward-facing jump that has 2½ rotations in the air.

At the time, all of the best skaters were doing single Axels. In fact, Button had never even tried the double Axel in competition until the 1948 Winter Games. But Button was daring. He pushed himself to be the best.

US figure skater Dick Button shows off a jump during a practice at the 1948 Olympic Winter Games in St. Moritz, Switzerland.

At 18, he was already one of the top skaters in the world. And his gamble paid off. The double Axel helped Button become the United States' first Olympic figure skating champion.

A Jumping Star

No one knew then how important that jump was. Figure skating looked much different in the 1930s and 1940s. Today, the top men's figure skaters attempt quadruple jumps. That means they do four rotations in the air. That is possible because of Button. He was the man who brought

Evan Lysacek

Dick Button set a high standard for US male figure skaters. Evan Lysacek did his best to match that standard at the 2010 Winter Games in Vancouver, Canada. Lysacek finished with a score of 257.67 points overall. He defeated 2006 gold medalist Evgeni Plushenko of Russia by just 1.31 points. It was a milestone victory for the United States. Skaters from Russia had won the men's gold medal at every Winter Games since 1992. The last US man to win figure skating gold was Brian Boitano in 1988. One area Lysacek did not follow Button in was risk taking. The Illinois native performed a clean routine, but he did not join Plushenko in performing a difficult quad jump. In a different way, however, that risk paid off. "I saw that American flag go up and I couldn't believe it was for me," Lysacek said. "I'm still in shock right now. I wasn't prepared for this. Going into this season, I never planned to win the gold medal."

Dick Button, shown at a practice session for the 1948 Olympics, was known for his spectacular jumping abilities.

athleticism to the sport. In addition to the double Axel, he was the first to do other moves, such as the triple loop and camel spin.

But when Button was growing up, there was another part of the sport that many thought was as important as jumps, spins, and other moves in free skating. It was called compulsory figures. Figure skaters traced figure-8 designs into the ice. They did it by gliding on certain edges of their skate blades. Tracing figures was hard to do. It took a lot of balance to tilt the blade all the way around to make two circles. But it was also kind of boring to do—and watch.

Button liked free skating better. What he liked best, though, was performing to a musical program. Button began skating when he was a boy. He learned on hockey skates, not figure skates. He also played other sports such as football and baseball. When Button was 13, his father saw his potential as a figure skater and sent him to train with a famous coach from Switzerland. The boy was a quick learner.

In 1943, he placed second in the novice division at the Eastern States Championships. Later that year, he won the Middle Atlantic title.

Dutch Dominance

Speedskating has its origins in the Netherlands. Despite having a population of just 16.8 million, the Dutch have dominated long-track speedskating in the Olympics. The first big stars were Ard Schenk and Kees Verkerk. They combined to win four gold medals and four silver medals from 1964 to 1972. However, the Dutch were at their best at the 2014 Olympic Winter Games in Sochi, Russia. The Netherlands won 24 total medals. All but one of them came in long-track speedskating. The other? It was in short-track speedskating. Dutch skaters medaled in every long-track event. They swept the medals in four of 10 individual events. Plus the Dutch men and women each won the team pursuit events.

He then went on to win the men's novice title at the US championships in 1944. He followed that with the US junior title in 1945.

In 1946, Button became the youngest man to win the senior title at nationals. He was just 16 years old. The win was his first of seven US senior championships in a row.

Button knew he needed to be at his best to beat the best at the 1948 Olympics. The reigning world champion at the time was Hans Gerschwiler of Switzerland. Button had beaten Gerschwiler at the European Championships that year. However, the Swiss skater had beaten Button in the 1947 World Championships. Those championships were the first since 1939 due to World War II. Button wasn't going to back down from a challenge at the Olympics.

"When Dick goes into the air, he uses as much energy as a broad jumper," the publicity manager of the Boston Skating Club told the *Harvard Crimson* student newspaper in 1948.

Although he had practiced the double Axel, Button wasn't even planning on trying it until a couple of days before the Olympics. When he landed it in the free skate, he wasn't surprised by the reaction. Eight of the nine judges ranked him first. Through the 2014 Olympics, Button was still the youngest Olympic gold medalist in men's figure skating.

Four years later, Button won his second Olympic gold medal at the 1952 Winter Games in Oslo, Norway. No men's figure skater has won back-to-back gold medals since. However, most fans had to read about his victories in the newspaper or hear it on the radio. The Olympics weren't televised until 1956.

Button was the most famous figure skater of his time. But he might have become even more famous thanks to his later work as a figure skating commentator on television. He even received an Emmy Award for his television work in the 1980s.

"I didn't learn what skating was all about until after I had won two Olympic Games," he said.

Grenoble 1968
A STAR IS BORN

To skating fans tuning in on television, Peggy Fleming must have looked like a princess. The 1968 Olympic Winter Games in Grenoble, France, were noteworthy for women's figure skating. It was the first time the sport was televised live and in color at the Olympics. Viewers could watch the competition unfold from their living rooms.

Fleming was the perfect figure skater to introduce the beauty of the sport to the world. On the day she won the Olympic gold medal, the 19-year-old Californian moved

US figure skaters, *from left*, Tina Noyes, Janet Lynn, and Peggy Fleming pose for the cameras at the 1968 Olympic Winter Games in Grenoble, France.

across the ice like a ballet dancer in her light green skating outfit. Her performance wasn't flawless. But it didn't have to be.

Fleming's gracefulness and artistry matched perfectly with the television boom. She was the leader of a new era. She would help make figure skating more popular for years to come. Fleming's performance at the 1968 Olympics was significant for another reason. It helped heal a sport rocked by tragedy seven years earlier.

Tragedy Strikes US Team

Fleming was 12 years old and the best skater in her hometown when she heard the news. A plane carrying the US figure skating team to the World Championships crashed near Brussels, Belgium. All 73 people on the plane were killed that day in 1961. Among them was William Kipp. He had coached Fleming in Paramount, California.

"It was a huge, huge loss that cut off our sport at the knees," Fleming said later. "It took us awhile to rebuild the coaching staff and the talent because all those skaters were going to be the role models of the next generation."

When the team perished, it was left to others—namely, Fleming—to carry the torch for US skating.

"I was it," she said.

Big Skates to Fill

At the time, however, Fleming was too young to fully understand what had happened. It was only three years earlier that she had slipped on her first pair of skates at a local ice rink. But she was a natural. She loved the sport right away. Her mother sewed many of her skating dresses.

Fleming never won a national novice or junior title. But in 1964 at age 15, she entered her first US championships as a senior competitor. She went home with the gold medal. It was her first of five straight national titles. That same year, she participated in the 1964 Winter Games in

Tonya and Nancy

One of the strangest storylines in figure skating history didn't happen on the ice. US skaters Tonya Harding and Nancy Kerrigan were expected to compete for medals at the 1994 Olympics in Lillehammer, Norway. A few weeks earlier at the US championships, however, an attacker whacked Kerrigan in the knee after a practice session. Kerrigan recovered in time and was named to the Olympic team. But it turned out that Harding's ex-husband was behind the attack.

The story became an international scandal. CBS's primetime telecast of the Olympic short program was the third-highest rated sports event in television history. However, a little known Ukrainian skater named Oksana Baiul edged Kerrigan for the gold medal. Harding, meanwhile, finished eighth. She later admitted to having learned of the plot to attack Kerrigan after the fact and was banned for life from US figure skating.

Innsbruck, Austria. Fleming finished in sixth place, the best finish of any US skater.

The next season, her parents brought her to Colorado Springs, Colorado. She began training under a famous coach there named Carlo Fassi. Fleming worked hard to perfect a trademark move. It was a double Axel jump that began and ended from a spread eagle position.

The 1965 World Championships were in Colorado Springs. Fleming captured the bronze medal behind Petra Burka of Canada and Regine Heitzer of Austria. Then she came back the next year and won her first world title. She captured the 1967 world title as well, setting her up for Olympic glory in 1968.

If Fleming was nervous on the day of her 1968 Olympic free skate, she didn't show it. When she got the jitters, Fleming said she would play with her hair. She once said she must have used a whole can of hairspray on the day she was crowned Olympic champion. Once she stepped onto the ice, though, she carried herself with confidence.

Fleming had built up a large lead after the compulsory figures. However, her free skate was a bit shaky. Fleming turned a double Axel into a single and landed a double Lutz on two feet instead of one. Even so, she easily won all of the first-place votes from the judges.

Peggy Fleming shows off her gold medal from the 1968
Olympic Winter Games.

Fleming became the first US Olympic medalist since Carol Heiss won gold and Barbara Ann Roles won bronze at the 1960 Winter Games in Squaw Valley, California. The generation of skaters who were supposed to follow them died the next year in the plane crash. But after Fleming, a US woman won a figure skating medal in every Olympics through 2006.

Fleming's win also made her the only US gold-medal winner at the 1968 Games. Like Dick Button in the 1940s and 1950s, Fleming became an important figure of her era in the United States. Both have remained in the figure skating spotlight for years, working alongside each other as television commentators.

4

Calgary 1988
BATTLE OF
THE BRIANS

Brian Boitano stood at the boards, staring at his coach. He was moments away from his free skate. There was no need to say a word. The figure skater was ready.

The men's event at the 1988 Winter Games in Calgary, Canada, was so anticipated it was dubbed "The Battle of the Brians." And that name originated weeks before Boitano of the United States and Brian Orser of Canada set foot in the arena.

US figure skater Brian Boitano acknowledges the crowd after finishing his short program at the 1988 Olympic Winter Games in Calgary, Canada.

The competition between them was fierce. Their rivalry started at the 1984 Winter Games in Sarajevo, a city in present day Bosnia and Herzegovina. Orser won the silver medal that year while Boitano was fifth. Over the next four seasons, the skaters both won world championships. Both also had specialty jumps. For Orser, it was the triple Axel. For Boitano, it was the "Tano triple Lutz," a move he invented. It was performed with one arm above his head.

Orser won the short program in Calgary. But Boitano had done better in the compulsory figures. So going into the free skate, Boitano held a slim lead. Boitano took the ice before Orser in the long program. Writing in his autobiography later, Boitano said he heard his brother yell from the stands.

"Boitano!" one fan called out.

"Orser!" responded a fan of the Canadian Orser.

Many figure skaters dream of winning a gold medal. Boitano was about to experience it. Skating to the soundtrack from the 1927 movie *Napoleon*, Boitano landed his first jump—the Tano triple Lutz—with ease. Next up was his first combination, a triple Axel-double toe loop.

Done.

Then a triple flip. Done.

Brian Boitano touches his skates during a leap in the free skate at the 1988 Olympic Winter Games.

Fans in the arena could sense Boitano was closing in on something special. He then performed a triple Salchow, followed by a triple loop-triple toe combination. He drew a deep breath as he went into his spread eagle. Then came his last jump, a triple Axel. It was his second triple Axel of the night.

Boitano was excited when he finished. When his scores popped up on the scoreboard, he felt confident. He received five 5.9s (out of a possible 6.0) for technical merit. He earned three more for artistry.

Orser's Turn

When Orser took the ice, he was nervous. It was easy to understand. The Olympics were in Canada, and Orser was considered his country's only gold-medal hope. Boitano didn't watch Orser skate. He went to the dressing room and waited.

Orser didn't land his second planned triple Axel. He had to downgrade it to a double. Many thought his fate was sealed after that. Boitano had done two triple Axels. The triple Axel is one of the hardest jumps in skating. Orser also landed a triple flip on two feet, another error. When Orser's scores came up, the lead was Boitano's. He won in a 5–4 judges' decision.

In his book *Boitano's Edge*, the skater wrote that he had pulled off his headphones just as the arena announcer said one of Orser's scores: "6.0!" At that moment, Boitano thought he had lost. He wrote: "I walked over to the mirror and stared at my reflection. 'That's okay,' I thought. 'I skated

Soviet Pairs

The Soviet Union and later Russia have dominated Olympic pairs figure skating. From 1964 to 2014, Russian or Soviet teams won 13 gold medals in 14 Olympics. The team of Katya Gordeyeva and Sergey Grinkov might have been the best. They won the 1988 gold medal while competing for the Soviet Union. Later, as professionals, they were not allowed to compete in the 1992 Winter Games. However, the rules changed and the team returned in 1994 to win another gold medal. This time they were representing Russia. Their story ended in tragedy, however. In 1995, Grinkov was rehearsing for a professional show when he had a heart attack and died.

Gold medalist Brian Boitano, *center*, silver medalist Brian Orser, *left*, and bronze medalist Viktor Petrenko pose for the cameras at the 1988 Olympic Winter Games.

great. That's what counts. I can keep competing and aim for the next Olympics in four more years. That's okay.'"

Then one of his US teammates, Christopher Bowman, entered the dressing room and held up a finger: Number One. But there was still one more skater to perform: Viktor Petrenko of the Soviet Union. There was a chance, should Petrenko get one first-place vote, that Orser could still win. But it didn't happen.

Bowman stayed with Boitano in the locker room. In his book, Boitano wrote that he learned he had won from a US team doctor. The doctor opened the door and said, "You won! You won the gold medal!"

Silver, again, went to Orser. Petrenko won the bronze medal. He became the first Ukrainian to win a medal in an individual event at a Winter Olympics.

Boitano's victory was a lesson in hard work. He was a roller skater before a figure skater. He wore second-hand skates on the ice at first.

"I wasn't the most talented skater on the ice," he wrote in his book. "But I was athletic. All that roller-skating had probably helped my coordination, and I was a really hard worker. I stayed on the ice until they kicked me off. I loved getting better and better every day."

Battle of the Carmens

The Battle of the Brians in the men's event wasn't the only rivalry at the 1988 Olympics. The women's final featured the "Battle of the Carmens." But "Carmen" didn't refer to the skaters' first names. Instead it was the name of the music that American Debi Thomas and East Germany's Katarina Witt both had chosen for their free skate.

Witt was the favorite. She was the defending Olympic champion. Plus she had defeated Thomas at the 1987 World Championships. The two skaters hadn't competed against each other since.

Heading into the Calgary Games, Thomas had delivered performances and results that were groundbreaking. In 1986, during her freshman year

Katarina Witt of East Germany performs during the free skate at the 1988 Olympic Winter Games.

at Stanford University, she became the first black woman to win the US title. She also won gold at the World Championships that year.

Unlike the men's event at Calgary, the Olympic showdown between Thomas and Witt wasn't as exciting. Witt didn't skate her best. However, she won the gold medal and became the first skater since Sonja Henie in 1936 to successfully defend her Olympic title. Canadian Elizabeth Manley won the silver medal. Meanwhile, Thomas missed several jumps and won the bronze medal. But Thomas's performance made history. She was the first black athlete to win a medal in any sport at the Winter Olympics.

5

Lillehammer 1994
WORTH THE WAIT

One last chance for a medal. It was Dan Jansen against the clock. But really it was Dan Jansen against himself. The US long-track speedskater was in his fourth Olympic Winter Games, in 1994 in Lillehammer, Norway. It was his eighth and final Olympic race of his career. And now he was 1,000 meters away from making a lifelong dream come true.

Gold? Silver? Bronze? It didn't matter. Jansen had never won an Olympic medal. He was determined to win one—any color—in Lillehammer.

US speedskater Dan Jansen skates in the 1,000-meter race at the 1994 Olympic Winter Games in Lillehammer, Norway.

Jansen got into his starting position on the oval ice. It didn't matter who was in the lane next to him. It didn't matter that Jansen had seven world records and seven overall World Cup titles to his name. The World Cup is the top-level circuit of competitions each year. The past wasn't as important as the moment in front of him. The speedskater knew what he had to do.

Hard Times and Heartache

Others might have been thinking about Jansen's long and difficult journey. It began at the 1984 Winter Games in Sarajevo, Yugoslavia. Jansen finished fourth, just off the medal stand, in the 500 meters.

The Drive for Five

Eric Heiden might have been the best men's long-track speedskater in history. What he did at the 1980 Olympic Winter Games was remarkable. In a span of 10 days, Heiden won gold medals in all five events, including sprint and distance. He also set four Olympic records and one world record. Yet the Madison, Wisconsin, native went to the starting line of his final event in Lake Placid, New York, not knowing how he'd do. The night before, he had stayed up late to watch the US men's hockey team defeat the Soviet Union. That game later became known as "The Miracle on Ice." The victory must have inspired him. Heiden's winning time in the 10,000 meters was an amazing 6.20 seconds faster than the world record. He ended his Olympic career as the first person to win five individual gold medals in the same Olympics.

That wasn't a huge deal, though. Jansen was young. And he indeed went into the 1988 Olympics in Calgary, Canada, as a favorite. But he could hardly compete. He learned that his sister Jane had died of leukemia just before the 500 final.

The youngest of nine children, Dan Jansen had learned to skate at a young age because of his sister. His family grew up in West Allis, Wisconsin. By the time Dan was 16, he was a junior world-record holder in the 500 meters. A week before the 1988 Winter Games, Jansen was considered the best skater in the world after winning the World Sprint Championships.

But sadness was looming. He knew his sister was dying. He spoke to her on the phone on the morning of the 500. But he skated with a heavy heart. Early in the race, he slipped and fell. Four days later, he fell again in the finals of the 1,000. Although he didn't win a medal, he won the US Olympic Spirit Award for skating through tragedy.

Four years later, there was more sadness. Jansen again had high hopes going into the 1992 Winter Games in Albertville, France. But again he missed a medal in the 500, placing fourth. He was also twenty-sixth in the 1,000.

US speedskater Dan Jansen climbs to his feet after falling and being disqualified in the 500-meter race at the 1988 Olympic Winter Games in Calgary, Canada.

One Last Chance

The International Olympic Committee changed the Olympic schedule.

The next Winter Games would actually take place in 1994 instead of 1996.

That meant the Summer Games and Winter Games now fell in different

years. It also meant Jansen had one more chance for gold in Lillehammer.

Now here it was. And again, Jansen was one of the favorites. Four times between 1992 and 1994, he was the only man to break 36 seconds in the 500. Still, bad luck seemed to follow him to the Olympics. He slipped in the 500 meters—his best event—and took eighth. Four days later and with one last race to go, Jansen knew the odds were not good. Three previous times he competed in the 1,000 meters at the Olympics. Yet he never finished better than sixteenth.

How would he do? In his autobiography, *Full Circle*, Jansen wrote, "Suddenly, right before I heard the gun, a jolt of energy came into my legs. . . . I knew I was ready."

Right to Play

Norway's Johann Olav Koss proved to be one of the greatest long-track speedskaters of all time. He won a gold and a silver medal at the 1992 Olympics. But Koss cemented his legacy on home ice at the 1994 Winter Games in Lillehammer, Norway. There he won the 1,500-, 5,000-, and 10,000-meter races. He set two Olympic records and one world record. Koss's legacy includes more than skating, however. He donated his 1994 prize money to charity and challenged fellow Norwegians to donate as well. That led to him creating Right to Play. It is a charity that works to provide disadvantaged children around the world with an opportunity to play sports.

Dan Jansen skates a victory lap with his daughter Jane after winning the 1,000-meter race at the 1994 Olympic Winter Games.

Skating in the fourth pair, he dug his skate blades into the ice. With every turn, Jansen felt faster and in control. He was on world-record pace at 600 meters, until, suddenly, on the second to last turn, he slipped. Jansen's left hand brushed the ice, but he regained his balance. Driving through the finish line, he could hardly believe what he saw. He finished in 1 minute, 12.43 seconds, beating the world record by .11 seconds. Jansen won the gold medal!

After receiving his medal, he saluted the sky in honor of his late sister. And then, holding his eight-month-old daughter, Jane, he skated a victory lap around the oval. The moment provided one of the most-photographed images of the Winter Games. The US Olympic team honored Jansen by electing him to bear the American flag at the Closing Ceremony. His final Olympic competition truly was a race to remember.

6

Vancouver 2010
A NEW STANDARD IN SHORT-TRACK

On his final day as an active Olympian, Apolo Anton Ohno posted a message on one of his social media pages.

"It's time," he wrote. "Heart of a lion. I will give my all—heart, mind, & spirit today. This is what it's about! All the way until the end! No regrets!"

Ohno was pumping himself up for something big. The setting was the 2010 Olympic Winter Games in Vancouver, Canada. The race was the 5,000-meter relay. And Ohno was about to win his eighth medal

US short-track speedskater Apolo Anton Ohno leads his teammates in a practice at the 2010 Olympic Winter Games in Vancouver, Canada.

in short-track speedskating. No US winter Olympian had previously won so many medals. No short-track speedskater had won so many, either.

Two events earlier, Ohno had won a bronze medal in 1,000 meters. It was his seventh medal. That eclipsed the former record of six medals set by US long-track speedskater Bonnie Blair. She won five gold medals and one bronze in three Olympics (1988, 1992, and 1994).

Now Ohno was about to add one more to his collection. It would be his third medal in Vancouver. The Games were Ohno's third Olympics, and he was competing not far from where he grew up in Seattle, Washington.

Bonnie Blair's Amazing Run

It was the final Olympic race of Bonnie Blair's long-track speedskating career. And she went out with a flourish at the 1994 Olympic Winter Games in Lillehammer, Norway. Blair was paired with a rival skater from China. That gave her extra motivation to win the 1,000-meter race. And despite a slight slip at the halfway mark, she skated her fastest 600 split since the 1988 Olympics. Blair won in 1 minute, 18.74 seconds. No other skater broke 1:20. It was a fitting ending for Blair. Her six medals (five gold, one bronze) were a record for a US Winter Olympian until 2010. All of Blair's medals were won in individual events. She also became the first woman to win the 500 in three consecutive Olympics, in 1988, 1992, and 1994.

"She's been good since 1984," fellow US speedskater Eric Heiden told the *Chicago Tribune* in 1994. "It's a long, long time to stay on top of a sport like this. I sure couldn't do it myself."

It had been a remarkable journey for Ohno. He had an agile and compact body that was perfect for the sport. Short-track was introduced in the Olympics in 1992. Unlike long-track speedskating, where skaters race in pairs against the clock, short-track athletes race in a pack on a smaller, 111-meter oval. Turns are tight and skaters can't make body contact when they pass each other. Because a race can be filled with crashes, with athletes sliding into the boards, short-trackers wear helmets to protect themselves.

Rising to the Top

Success came early for Ohno. He was just 14 when he became the youngest US short-track champion in 1997. But Ohno didn't make the 1998 US Olympic team. He was sad and disappointed. There were 16 skaters at the Olympic Trials, and Ohno placed last.

It was tough, but Ohno vowed the experience would make him stronger. Raised by a single father, Ohno leaned on his dad for support. Step by step, Ohno got better. He began winning again. He became the overall champion at the 1999 Junior World Championships. Two years later, he won the World Cup title.

Ohno made his Olympic debut in 2002 in Salt Lake City, Utah. He won his first gold in the 1,500 meters. But the win was controversial.

Ohno crossed the finish line second but was moved up to first after the apparent winner—South Korea's Kim Dong-Sung—was disqualified. Judges ruled that the Korean skater had obstructed Ohno in the final turn.

Ohno also captured the silver medal in the 1,000 behind Steven Bradbury of Australia. In that race, Ohno slid into the boards but scurried across the finish line on his hands and knees to clinch second. The performance in Salt Lake City made Ohno a star. With his wavy brown hair, thick soul patch, and signature bandana often around his head, Ohno was hard to miss.

His star continued to rise at the 2006 Olympics in Turin, Italy. Ohno won three medals there. He won gold in the 500 meters. He added bronze medals in the 1,000 and the team relay.

Aussie Magic

In his three Olympics, Australian Steven Bradbury had never finished higher than eighth in an individual short-track event. Then he stepped on the ice for the men's 1,000-meter finals at the 2002 Winter Games in Salt Lake City, Utah. Bradbury rarely skated out into the lead in races. But he advanced through the quarterfinals and semifinals because skaters in front of him fell or were disqualified. In the finals, it happened again. Bradbury was the last man standing when four skaters tumbled to the ice in a race to the finish line. As they slid into the boards, Bradbury skated across the finish line as the gold medalist. It was the first time a non-Korean had won the event.

Apolo Anton Ohno, *right*, struggles to cross the finish line after a fall during the final stretch of the 1,000-meter race at the 2002 Olympic Winter Games.

Ohno's Olympic swansong would come just north of his hometown in Vancouver. He began by winning a silver medal in the 1,500 and a bronze medal in the 1,000. Ohno was also favored to win his third race and repeat as the 500-meter champion. But on the final turn at the Pacific Coliseum, he was disqualified. Judges ruled that Ohno interfered with another skater on the final turn of the final lap.

As he raced past reporters waiting to interview him, Ohno didn't stop. He just reminded them that he had "one chance left" to extend his record to eight medals in the team relay.

J. R. Celski, Travis Jayner, and Jordan Malone joined Ohno on the 5,000-meter relay team. Fittingly, Ohno skated the anchor leg. He led Team USA to a bronze medal, behind Canada and South Korea. But to Ohno, third place felt like first.

"It was really a team effort," Ohno told reporters in a news conference after the race. "Without these guys, I wouldn't be able to skate individually."

Ohno was such a popular Olympian after the 2006 Winter Games that he was invited to compete on the TV show *Dancing with the Stars* in 2007. To no one's surprise, Ohno won that, too.

Vancouver 2010
GOLD FOR
THE QUEEN

In South Korea, she's known simply as "Queen Yuna." Even before she stood on the gold-medal podium at the 2010 Olympic Winter Games in Vancouver, Canada, Yuna Kim was her country's most popular female athlete. Everywhere she went, camera shutters clicked and microphones captured her every word.

When Kim skated onto the ice for her long program in Vancouver, more than half of her country's 48 million people were watching on television. She was

South Korean figure skater Yuna Kim performs during the free skate at the 2010 Olympic Winter Games in Vancouver, Canada.

about to give them one of the all-time best performances in Olympic figure skating.

"I can't believe this day has finally come for me," she said.

Heading into the free skate, Kim's lead was fewer than five points over Mao Asada of Japan. They were rivals since their days as junior skaters. Now both 19, Kim knew that Asada was the only skater capable of challenging her for the gold medal.

"It's not any time to hold back," Kim's coach, two-time Olympic men's silver medalist Brian Orser, told reporters. "It's not a time to be conservative or cautious. Be Olympic. We've talked about that coming here."

The Queen Reigns

Kim skated first. Wearing a royal blue dress and performing to Gershwin's "Concerto in F," she landed six triple jumps. Among them was a triple Lutz-triple toe loop combination. All of her jumps would receive positive marks from the judges.

When she finished, gifts of flowers and stuffed animals rained down from the stands. Orser shook his fists in the air like a boxing champion. By the time she returned to the boards to greet him, Kim was in tears. Never before had she cried after a performance, she said.

Yuna Kim dazzled fans at the 2010 Olympic Winter Games with her tremendous performance in the free skate.

"I honestly don't know why I cried," Kim said. "Maybe I was relieved. Maybe I was satisfied with my performance."

Maybe she was perfect. The judges gave her a world-record score of 150.06 for the long program. Her total was 228.56, another world record.

"I predicted that my score [in the long program] would probably be 140," Kim said. "I still can't believe that score. I'm really surprised. It's close to a men's score. I was afraid I wouldn't be able to do what I wanted. But I was happy to show everything I did in training."

But the competition wasn't over. Asada still had to skate. The 2008 world champion landed two triple Axels. However, she stumbled on her footwork leading into her triple toe and didn't complete the jump. Skating to Rachmaninoff's "Bells of Moscow," Asada landed four clean triple jumps. But that was two fewer than Kim. Asada also didn't do either a triple Lutz or a triple toe.

When she finished her program, Asada knew it was over. It didn't matter that she became the first woman to land two triple Axels in one Olympic performance.

Go Team

Team figure skating made its Olympic debut in 2014. Each country performed a short and long program in men's, women's, pairs, and ice dancing. Scores were determined by each skater's rank in their category. The Russians shined on their home ice. Fifteen-year-old Yulia Lipnitskaya dazzled fans with her fast spins. Evgeni Plushenko, a gold medalist in 2006 and silver medalist in 2002 and 2010, returned from a long break to win the men's free skate and finish second in the short program. Meanwhile, Russian pairs teams also won both the short program and the free skate. Those performances pushed the home country to a gold medal over Canada and Team USA.

"I did everything I can," she said. "To complete both triple Axels well at the Olympics was one good thing about my performance. But I am not happy with the rest of my performance."

As Asada's marks popped up on the scoreboard, it showed that Kim had won the Olympic gold medal by a whopping 23.06 points over silver medalist Asada, who finished with 205.50. Kim's score was so good it would have placed her ninth in the men's competition. Joannie Rochette of Canada, skating four days after the death of her mother, won the bronze.

The US women went home without a medal for only the second time since 1952. The other time was 1964. That was three years after the plane crash claimed the lives of the 1961 US team as the squad traveled to the World Championships.

Kim's gold medal was South Korea's first at a Winter Olympics in a sport other than speedskating. She also became the second straight female skater from an Asian country to win the Olympic women's title. At the 2006 Winter Games in Turin, Italy, Shizuka Arakawa was Japan's first Olympic gold medalist.

But unlike Arakawa, Kim's victory was expected. She was the reigning world champion and biggest favorite since Katarina Witt in 1988. Entering

Yuna Kim stands on the podium after winning a gold medal at the 2010 Olympic Winter Games.

the Olympics, Kim had lost just one competition since finishing third at the 2008 World Championships.

As Kim bent to accept her gold medal in Vancouver, the tears began coming again. Her lip quivered. She started to cry as the South Korean anthem was played. After it was over, someone handed her a flag and she held it over her head as she skated a victory lap on the ice.

"I still can't believe it," Kim said. "I waited a long time for the Olympics, and it feels like a large weight has been lifted off."

Coming Up Silver

Four years later, at age 23, Kim returned to Olympic ice in Sochi, Russia. After Vancouver, she had little to prove. But Kim wanted to become the first woman to successfully defend her Olympic title since Witt in 1984 and 1988. However, it wasn't to be.

Kim won the short program but was defeated in the free skate by Russia's Adelina Sotnikova. Skating on home ice, Sotnikova captured the gold medal with 224.59 total points to Kim's 219.11. With the victory, Sotnikova became Russia's first women's Olympic champion.

Dancing to Victory

They trained at the same rink in Michigan. They even trained under the same coach. At the 2010 Olympics, Canadian ice dancers Tessa Virtue and Scott Moir won gold while Americans Meryl Davis and Charlie White took silver. But the positions began changing soon after.

The dynamic and athletic team of Davis and White had been competing together since elementary school. They came into the 2014 Olympics as world champions. And in Sochi, Russia, they bested their training rivals easily to give the United States its first Olympic gold medal in ice dancing. The couple set a new record score with 195.52 points. Virtue and Moir earned silver with 190.99. Ice dance had been accepted into the Olympics in 1976. However, European teams long dominated the sport. Ice dancing gained popularity in North America when the US team of Tanith Belbin and Ben Agosto won the Olympic silver medal in 2006.

Great
Olympians

Viktor Ahn
(South Korea and Russia)

The Russian short-track speedskater won three gold medals and a bronze in 2014, matching his feat from 2006 when he was representing South Korea.

Lyudmila Belousova and Oleg Protopopov (Soviet Union)

Known for their famous death spiral, this pairs figure skating team won gold in 1964 and 1968.

Bonnie Blair (USA)

She is the only long-track speedskater to win an event three times, claiming the 500 gold medal in 1988, 1992, and 1994. She also won two gold medals and a bronze in the 1,000.

Dick Button (USA)

He won figure skating gold medals in 1948 and 1952 while introducing athleticism and big jumps to the sport.

Eric Heiden (USA)

He won five gold medals in five events at the 1980 Winter Games, setting Olympic or world records in each win.

Sonja Henie (Norway)

She was a three-time Olympic figure skating champion (1928, 1932, 1936) and a pioneer with her outfits and choreography.

Yuna Kim (South Korea)

"Queen Yuna" dazzled fans with her gold-medal figure skating performance in 2010, and then won a silver medal in 2014.

Apolo Anton Ohno (USA)

The short-track speedskater won a record eight medals from 2002 to 2010, two of them gold.

Claudia Pechstein (Germany)

With nine medals, including five gold, from 1992 to 2006, she is the most decorated Olympic long-track speedskater.

Glossary

AXEL

A jump in which the figure skater takes off from the forward outside edge and lands on the back outside edge of the opposite foot. The jump is named for its creator, Axel Paulsen.

COMBINATION JUMPS

Figure skating jumps in which each subsequent jump takes off from the same landing edge of the preceding jump. There can be no turns or steps in between the jumps. Combinations usually consist of two jumps.

COMPULSORY FIGURES

Steps, turns, and edges performed on specific points on the ice. The Olympic figure skating competition used to include a round of compulsory figures.

FREE SKATE

Also known as the long program, the free skate does not have required elements. Figure skaters display their technical and artistic skills in a four-minute routine.

INTERFERENCE

In short-track speedskating, this violation is called if a skater is at fault for obstructing or colliding with another skater.

LUTZ

A toe-pick-assisted jump taken off from a back outside edge and landed on the back outside edge of the opposite foot.

PACK STYLE

In short-track speedskating, up to six skaters compete at once, not confined to lanes, using race strategies.

SHORT PROGRAM

A 2:50-minute program in singles and pairs figure skating that consists of seven required elements. It precedes the free skate.

TOE LOOP

A toe-pick-assisted figure skating jump that takes off and lands on the same back outside edge.

For More
Information

SELECTED BIBLIOGRAPHY

Hines, James R. *Figure Skating: A History*. Champaign, IL: University of Illinois Press, 2006.

US Figure Skating. *U.S. Figure Skating Media Guide*. USA: US Figure Skating, 2011-12.

Wallechinsky, David, and Jaime Loucky. *The Complete Book of the Winter Olympics: 2010 Edition*. London, UK: Aurum Press 2009.

FURTHER READINGS

Browning, Kurt. *A is for Axel: An Ice Skating Alphabet*. Chelsea, MI: Sleeping Bear Press, 2006.

Judd, Ron C. *The Winter Olympics: An Insider's Guide to the Legends, the Lore, and the Games: Vancouver Edition*. Seattle, WA: Mountaineers Books, 2009.

Milton, Steve. *Figure Skating's Greatest Stars*. Richmond Hill, ON: Firefly Books, 2009.

WEBSITES

To learn more about Great Moments in Olympic Sports, visit **booklinks.abdopublishing.com**. These links are routinely monitored and updated to provide the most current information available.

PLACES TO VISIT

US and World Figure Skating Museum and Hall of Fame
20 First Street
Colorado Springs, Colorado 80906
(719) 635-5200
www.worldskatingmuseum.org
The World Figure Skating Museum is dedicated to the preservation of figure skating history. The US and World Halls of Fame are also located at US Figure Skating headquarters. It is open to the public year-round.

US Olympic Training Center
1750 E Boulder St.
Colorado Springs, CO 80909
(719) 866-4618
www.teamusa.org
The US Olympic team has welcomed more than 1.6 million visitors to its headquarters in Colorado Springs, Colorado. In addition to extensive training facilities for elite athletes, the USOTC offers visitors the chance to discover US Olympic history through its indoor and outdoor exhibitions and installations. Walking tours are conducted daily.

Index

ABOUT THE AUTHOR

Award-winning journalist Jo-Ann Barnas has travelled to more than a dozen countries covering international sporting events, including eight Olympic Games. She worked at the *Detroit Free Press* from 1995 to 2012. She was voted 2005 Michigan Sportswriter of the Year by the National Sportscasters and Sportswriters Association. Other top honors include two national first-place APSE awards. Barnas began her professional career in 1984 at the *Kansas City Star*.